D

27

GW00640747

E20455

Smile

A play for women

David Campton

Samuel French – London
New York – Sydney – Toronto – Hollywood

CHARACTERS

Grandmama — in her late sixties or early seventies, with a sharp mind and an iron will

Mama — a vague person about fifty, accustomed to being ignored

Millicent — in her late twenties or early thirties, spoiled and repressed

Matilda — Millicent's twin. Not identical in looks, but with a personality that is almost interchangeable with her sister

Alice — a maid, younger than the twins, knows her place but has a mind of her own

The action takes place in a sunlit garden in the afternoon

Time— the second half of the nineteenth century

NOTES

The twins and Alice may be played up to ten years older than described, as long as the ages of Mama and Grandmama, and the number of years since Mama's lapse, are adjusted accordingly.

There could be a change of lighting as characters retire into their own thoughts, but this is not mandatory.

SMILE

A sunny afternoon in a large garden with a background of trees and bushes. The second half of the nineteenth century

A small, slow procession enters. At the head is Grandmama, relying heavily on a thick stick and Mama's arm. They are followed by Millicent and Matilda, each carrying two chairs

Grandmama This is all so unnecessary.

Mama When one considers the subject carefully, one comes to the conclusion that hardly anything proves to be absolutely necessary.

Grandmama Photographs! Why photographs?

Millicent On account of ...

Matilda ... your birthday, Grandmama. And because we ...

Millicent ... do not have a likeness that does not ...

Matilda ... date back thirty years ... We want to ...

Millicent ... remember you just as we ...

Matilda ... remember you now.

Millicent ⎱ (*speaking together*) Tilly!
Matilda ⎰ Milly!

Millicent ⎱ (*speaking together*) You are taking words out of my
Matilda ⎰ mouth again.

Grandmama Stop!

Mama Here, Mama?

Millicent So close ...

Matilda ... to the house?

Mama Indeed the furniture appears almost embarassed at finding itself in the open air, as though surprised by bailiffs.

Millicent Why not the *summer*-house?

Matilda I was about to suggest the summer-house.

Millicent Then I saved you the trouble.

Matilda I'll thank you to let me speak for myself.

Grandmama Not the summer-house.

Millicent Why not, Grandmama?

Grandmama Because I said not the summer-house. Here.

Mama If you say so, Mama.

The twins start to set the chairs in a row

Grandmama Set them this way.
Matilda But then we shall be facing the house.
Millicent Surely you would rather view the garden.
Grandmama I turned my back on the garden years ago. Leave it where it is.
Millicent }
Matilda } *(speaking together)* But, Grandmama ...
Grandmama Does either of you have a cogent reason why we should *not* face the house?
Millicent }
Matilda } *(speaking together)* No, Grandmama.
Grandmama Then seat me.
Millicent }
Matilda } *(speaking together)* Yes, Grandmama.

The twins help Grandmama on to one of the two centre chairs, which is turned round for the purpose. Then the other chairs are turned

Mama *(looking into the distance)* Alice apears to be approaching with a person who, from his impedementa, would appear to be a photographer.

As usual, Grandmama and the twins ignore her

Millicent Can you see the house from there, Grandmama?
Grandmama A gothic pile two hundred yards away? Should I *not* see it?
Matilda I believe Millicent intended to ask if you could see *into* the house.
Grandmama Why this sudden preoccupation with my faculties? I can see as much as needs to be seen, and a little more.

Alice enters and bobs deferentially

Alice Ma'am, the man.
Grandmama Man? *(With an imperious hand she halts the Photographer just out of view)*
Grandmama Sir! Keep your distance. Males are not encouraged on these premises.
Millicent Which is why the photograph must be taken out here.

Matilda In the garden.

Grandmama Is that the only reason?

Millicent What other reason ...

Matilda ... could there be?

Grandmama I've a suspicious mind, thank the Lord. .... All right, man. Do what you are paid to do. .... Eh? ... What is the idiot mumbling?

Alice If you please ma'am, he says will the ladies be so good as to dispose themselves.

Grandmama And what does that amount to in English?

Alice I think he wants you all to sit down, ma'am.

Grandmama Hear that? Dispose yourselves.

Millicent My chair, I think.

Matilda I put it there.

Grandmama Without argument.

Millicent
Matilda } *(speaking together)* Yes, Grandmama ...

They sit on either side of Grandmama, leaving a chair free at the end of the row

Grandmama You, too, Juliet.

Mama I feel strangely excited, as though something unprecedentedly momentous were about to occur. An almost forgotten sensation ...

Grandmama Sit.

Mama Yes, Mama. *(She sits on the remaining chair)* It being so long since anything momentously unprecedented happened to me ...

Millicent Oh!

Mama Or if it ever did ...

Matilda But ...

Mama ... having completely slipped my memory.

Millicent
Matilda } *(speaking together)* Alice!

Alice Yes, miss?

Millicent What is to be done ...

Matilda ... about Alice?

Millicent She must be ...

Matilda ... in the picture, too.

Alice Me, miss?

Grandmama Maidservant and mistress in the same photograph?
  What is the world coming to?
Alice I hope I know my place better than that, ma'am.
Millicent Your place is with us, Alice.
Matilda As an old retainer.
Alice Old, miss?
Matilda Retainer, anyway.
Millicent And if you wish to be retained . . .
Matilda You will join us in the photograph.
Alice I really ought to go back into the house, miss.
Millicent Why?
Matilda Indeed.
Alice While I'm here, I can't be there.
Millicent So?
Alice To answer the door, miss. If anybody should call.
Millicent Are you expecting a call, Matilda?
Matilda Not this afternoon, Millicent.
Millicent So, join us, Alice.
Alice I couldn't, miss.
Grandmama Couldn't? What language is that, girl?
Alice I don't care for things being pointed at me, ma'am. Specially
  when I can't see who's pointing what.
Mama For why is the man taking cover under a black cloth?
Grandmama If I am equal to facing that contraption, why not
  you?
Alice But, ma'am . . .
Grandmama Are you contradicting, girl?
Alice Oh no, ma'am.
Grandmama Then assume a respectful attitude for the photog-
  rapher.
Alice Where, ma'am?
Grandmama Anywhere inconspicuous.
Alice Yes, ma'am.

Alice stands next to Mama

Grandmama What is the man muttering now?
Alice He says the exposure will take a little time, ma'am.
Grandmama Exposure?
Alice He says: "Smile", "Hold it", "Don't move".

*The sitters freeze with fixed smiles. While they remain immobile,
Alice "unfreezes", steps forward and speaks in the direction of the
audience*

Being photographed was never part of my duties. Making beds,
yes. Making tea, making fires, making do, making anything
else—as long as it wasn't eyes at the grocer's boy. Men are not
allowed in this house. Even the chimney sweep was regarded
with suspicion—and he was only ten. My, how this photographer chap huffed and puffed when he had to make his way
round by the stable yard! "Lacking respect due to an artist", he
grumbled. "Would they have directed Holbein or Gainsbor-
ough round by the stable?" he wanted to know. I told him if
they were men, they'd be lucky to get that far; but he went on "I
can catch a likeness more like than any old master". I wonder
what he meant by that—catch. What did he mean by exposure?
Our faces show what we're thinking, don't they? What may be
exposed on that picture? What can I do about it, anyway? Think
of nothing and smile. (*She goes back to her place, smiling and
standing stiffly*)

As she does so, Mama relaxes and comes forward

Mama How peaceful to pose like the lady in the painting (whose
name escapes me) with nothing expected of one but a smile;
leaving one at liberty to think—as far as one is able ... What
was the name of that lady? Something Italian if memory serves.
... If only memory would. Serve. If only one could recall what
really happened, long ago, when one woke up to discover that
one had given birth to twins. With no recollection of how they
came about. If the shock were enough to make one forget the
events leading up to it, what a great shock it must have been.
One may have been assured there had been a husband, acciden-
tally drowned on honeymoon in Italy like the poet, Shelley. Yet,
although one can remember what is reputed to have happened
to the poet, Shelley, one has no recollection whatever of
husband or honeymoon. Which must have been of short
duration, because one's command of Italian is so uncertain.
What one was told must have been true, because there is no
denying the twins. However dearly one would wish to ... They
are up to something. They are always up to something—usually

quite horrid—and take no more notice of one than if one were one of their dolls. Though what they did to their dolls doesn't bear dwelling on. What a pity *they* can't have honeymoons in Italy ... Unruly thoughts! Better think of nothing and smile. I wonder what *they* are thinking. (*She goes back to her place, sits, smiles and stiffens*)

The twins relax and come forward, keeping the width of the row of chairs between them

Millicent
Matilda } (*speaking together*) Take care.

Millicent What you think.

Matilda Because that one ...

Millicent ... could be thinking ...

Matilda ... the same.

Millicent
Matilda } (*speaking together*) Not so excited!

Millicent It would never do to let certain persons suspect ...

Matilda ... that one is involved with ...

Millicent ... well—what one is involved with.

Matilda What if she suspects already!

Millicent
Matilda } (*speaking together*) She mustn't!

Millicent She agreed so readily.

Matilda She'd never have agreed if she'd suspected.

Millicent Given half a chance to object.

Matilda She never agrees—which is suspicious.

Millicent Am I thinking her thoughts!

Matilda Is she thinking mine?

Millicent How provoking to have been born a biological joke.

Matilda To be half of two instead of one alone.

Millicent Siamese twins could not be more firmly linked.

Matilda A private life is impossible with her about.

Millicent But that will soon be done with.

Matilda As long as everyone can be kept away from the house.

Millicent Until it is all over.

Matilda (*smugly*) This time I shall strike first.

Millicent Quickly. Decisively.

Millicent
Matilda } (*speaking together*) Before *she* finds out.

The twins resume their seats. Grandmama relaxes

Grandmama Smile! Huh! Why are they doing this to me? Not for
love, that's certain. The noxious pair never had a generous
impulse between them. The young witches must always be
brewing up something. But what? Ah! Could nasty Nature be
asserting itself? After nearly thirty years? Ridiculous. Besides,
there are no men hereabouts. When was the last admitted? Over
twenty years ago: and he merely the doctor, certifying the cause
of Cedric's death as drink and delusions. Even tradesmen are
never allowed nearer than the tradesmen's entrance. Until this—
this—tradesman with his "Dispose yourselves, ladies" and
"Smile". We are in his hands because he is the only one who can
tell what we look like. A dangerous precedent. Give in to one
male whim and the way is wide open to total surrender, with all
its consequences. Ah! Better not recall that disaster. No, indeed.
Remember what remembering did to Cedric—taking to brandy
and seeing things. Did he take to drink because he saw things, or
did he see things because he took to drink? . . . Oh. Oh! (*She
slowly rises and points, tottering a few steps towards the house*)
Who—is—that?

*Startled, everyone forgets to pose. The twins jump up and take a few
steps in the direction of Grandmama's accusing finger*

Millicent What?
Matilda Where?
Grandmama There. There. There.

*Behind her, the twins make shooing gestures at the window, catch
each other doing it and change the gesture to something else—
patting hair, waving off flies, etc.*

Mama Is it all over? (*She stands and smiles vaguely around her*)
The process is less of an ordeal than I anticipated.
Alice (*moving to the Photographer*) You'll have to speak up, sir. I
can't hear a word with all this going on.
Grandmama At the window.
Millicent
Matilda (*speaking together*) Which window?
Alice (*to the Photographer*) Oh. Really?
Grandmama I saw.

Millicent }
Matilda } *(speaking together)* What?

Grandmama A—a . . .

Millicent }
Matilda } *(speaking together)* Oh, no, Grandmama.

Millicent Sunlight, perhaps

Matilda Reflections, maybe.

Grandmama I know what I saw.

Millicent Not a man, Grandmama.

Matilda There is no-one left in the house.

Millicent Certainly not a young man.

Matilda Men are not allowed.

Millicent Young or otherwise.

Matilda So you could never have seen one at the window.

Millicent A passing cloud, do you suppose?

Matilda A bird?

Grandmama I recognised . . .

Millicent A branch.

Matilda A trick of the light.

Grandmama I *thought* I recognized . . .

Alice *(to the Photographer)* I'll tell them.

Grandmama You saw nothing, you say?

Millicent }
Matilda } *(speaking together)* Absolutely nothing

Alice Ma'am . . .

Grandmama H'm. Assist me back.

The twins help her to her chair

Did *I* mention a young man?

Mama I recall Papa at times being convinced he had seen a young man. But was not that apparition usually in the vicinity of the summer-house? Beside, Papa was never able to verify his experiences with corroborative detail on account of the quantity of brandy consumed after such encounters. I wonder, though . . . *(As no-one is listening to her, her voice trails away)*

Alice If you please, ma'am . . .

Grandmama Well?

Alice The photographer says you moved.

Grandmama I am aware of the fact. I was moved to move.

Alice He says moving spoils the picture, ma'am. You'll come out like ghosts.

Grandmama Like what?
Alice Faint and fuzzy.
Millicent I am sure Grandmama would never come out faint.
Matilda Or fuzzy.
Alice He says, please to pose again.
Grandmama Does he indeed!
Alice And this time not to move, no matter what you see. Or think you see. Or . . .
Grandmama Any further commands from on high?
Alice Any? . . . Oh, yes, ma'am. . . . He says, "Smile, please".

The ladies resume their poses and smile

Millicent (*through her smile*) How long?
Matilda (*grinning unhappily*) As long as necessary.
Millicent (*still showing her teeth*) How long is necessary?
Matilda (*with fixed grin*) Till the deed is done.
Millicent What deed?

While the others are frozen, Alice relaxes

Alice Off their heads, if truth were told. But I must be as mad as the rest or I'd never have stayed with them. With their "Alice, do this". "Alice, do the other". "Alice why isn't it done already?" Especially when my name isn't Alice. "Who ever heard of a maid called Myfanwy?" said the old one. "While you are here you will answer to Alice". And so I shall. As long as I'm here. (*She resumes her position and smiles*)

Mama relaxes

Mama Did Mama truly observe a face? Or was it an airy nothing, merely reminding her of a face at the window? I could not be certain of my own senses, yet what I saw—or did not see as the case may be—suggested an occurrence long ago and, until now, quite forgotten. Oh, this ridiculous memory of mine! This wretched emptiness that refuses to be satisfied and that others try to fill with Italy. Why should the word Italy not remind me of blue skies, ruins, poets or even spaghetti, but connect rather with a shrubbery? (*Slightly surprised*) Oh . . . Why should anything glimpsed at a window also put me in mind of a shrubbery? . . . Could memory be returning at last after sleeping for so many years? Do I want it to? (*She resumes her position*)

The twins relax

Millicent } *(speaking together)* Him!
Matilda

Millicent At the window.

Matilda In the house now.

Millicent } *(speaking together)* My secret.
Matilda

Millicent We met in the shrubbery.

Matilda In the summer-house.

Millicent And continued to meet.

Matilda Repeatedly.

Millicent But how careless of him to be seen at the window.

Matilda When he should be burgling the house.

Millicent Only after the valuables have been secured ...

Matilda The silver.

Millicent The miniatures.

Matilda The cash box.

Millicent *Then* we can run away.

Matilda Together.

Millicent } *(speaking together)* Bliss!
Matilda

Millicent How silly of her to agree to the photograph.

Matilda She *is* silly.

Millicent As stupid as she is spiteful.

Matilda As spiteful as she is greedy.

Millicent } *(speaking together)* Why *did* she agree?
Matilda

Millicent Could she know about us?

Matilda She couldn't know about him.

Millicent About the theft.

Matilda About the elopement.

Millicent If she did, she would never have agreed.

Millicent } *(speaking together)* Would she?
Matilda

Millicent What is she thinking now?

Matilda Don't think of it.

Millicent Think of something totally ridiculous and irrelevant to confuse her.

Matilda Think of toasted muffins.

Millicent Think of a runcible spoon.

Matilda What is a runcible spoon?
Millicent Whatever that is.
Matilda And why should I be thinking of it? Is she thinking of something totally ridiculous and irrelevant to baffle me?
Millicent Where do muffins come in?
Matilda Does she guess?
Millicent How much does she know?
Matilda Does it matter?
Millicent Who cares as long as everyone is kept away from the house.
Matilda Until the signal.
Millicent Just wait for the signal.
Matilda Watch for the signal.
Millicent
Matilda } (*speaking together*) When it comes.

They resume their fixed positions. Grandmama relaxes

Grandmama What *was* at the window? Am I seeing things as Cedric did? Why, after all these years? I never did before—not even when Cedric was babbling into his cups like some remorseful villain in a second-rate melodrama. I am made of stronger stuff. Besides, I saw the young man laid to rest. Behind the shrubbery. I must admit I have never much cared to sit in the summer-house since—in spite of the fact that petunias flourish more brilliantly on that patch than anywhere else in the garden. A fertile patch. What Cedric saw, or thought he saw, thereafter is irrelevant. Young men put down as deeply as that one was do not pop up again in summer-houses. Or anywhere else. Such as windows. . . . My goodness how one's arms ache after shovelling earth. Such a pity Cedric had to hit the booby with a knobbly walking stick. Such a pity there wasn't a horse-whip to hand. Horse-whips are traditional and seldom fatal. But there wasn't a horse whip in the house and Cedric invariably carried a knobbly walking stick. What can a father be expected to do when he comes upon a young bounder doing what that young bounder was doing with one's daughter in the summer-house behind the shrubbery? Having lived with the memory for thirty years and never having once seen the young man's ghost, why begin now? No, I'll not admit it. If he should appear again—at the window or anywhere else—I'll give no sign of recognition. Cut him dead for the upstart he is. Was. Is. I'll not even call for my smelling salts. (*Pause, then shouting*) Where are my smelling salts?

The pose is broken as everyone turns to Grandmama

Millicent (*speaking together*) Smelling salts?
Matilda Why smelling salts?
Mama Are you ill?

Millicent Are you sure you want smelling salts, Grandmama?
Grandmama Why else would I call for smelling salts?
Matilda Fresh air is better if one is feeling faint.
Grandmama I am not feeling faint and I've had my fill of fresh air.
Mama Why is the photographer doing the Highland Fling?
Alice I'll ask, ma'am.
Matilda I'll fetch your vinaigrette, Grandmama.
Millicent Why should *you* fetch Grandmama's vinaigrette?
Matilda Because she is asking for it.
Alice The photographer says you moved again. He wants to know if you're doing it on purpose.
Grandmama Ask him what business that is of his.
Alice Yes, ma'am. . . . Oh, he heard you. He wants to know who is going to pay for the spoiled plates.
Grandmama That is his problem.
Alice He says . . .
Grandmama Let him say on. I am still waiting for those smelling salts.
Alice At once, ma'am.
Millicent No need. I'll go.
Matilda Oh, no. I'll go.
Millicent I said, I'll go.
Matilda Why say, "I'll go" when you can see I intend to go?
Millicent I said, "I'll go" because I can see you intend to go.
Matilda If you go, I go.
Millicent You'll not go without me going with you.
Matilda Two persons are not required to carry one smelling bottle.
Grandmama No one need go. I'll return to the house myself.

Grandmama rises. Alarmed, the twins urge her back into her seat

Millicent You can't!
Matilda Not yet!

Grandmama Why not?

Millicent The photograph.

Matilda You must stay for that.

Millicent We must *all* stay for that.

Matilda All?

Millicent All.

Alice The photographer wants to know if he is to try again.

Mama Yes, indeed. Photography was not so advanced in my late husband's time. Which may account for there being no likeness left. When one is unable to recall so much as a single feature one is inclined to wonder ... I mean there comes a time when a photograph is the only proof that one ever existed.

Grandmama Alice!

Alice At once, ma'am.

Alice hurries off

Millicent (*panicking*) If Alice goes back to the house now ...

Matilda (*firmly avoiding a dangerous suggestion*) She will not be on the photograph.

Grandmama Good. The rest of you sit. Wait. Smile.

Everyone sits. When they speak they continue to look ahead, immersed in their own thoughts

Millicent What can be done now?

Matilda Nothing can be done now.

Millicent But sit and wait.

Matilda Wait for Alice to scream.

Millicent For the inevitable commotion.

Matilda When rooms are found ransacked.

Millicent With all that is portable and valuable bundled up.

Matilda The perpetrator discovered on the premises.

Millicent In *flagrante dilicto*.

Matilda Red-handed.

Millicent Alice will not be used to dealing with criminal activity.

Matilda Even when committed by such a personable thief.

Millicent }
Matilda } (*speaking together*) So what now?

Mama Was that a young man's face? Or a mere imperfection in the glass? Did I really, however fleetingly, recognize those features?

Grandmama I've never believed in ghosts and don't intend to start now. Give me the smelling salts every time. It's a stubborn ghost that can stand up to a whiff of ammonia.

Mama Perhaps I was merely reminded of a face I wished to see again—the original having vanished into oblivion like a faded photograph. Such a persuasive young man. Not memorably handsome, for no memory remains of hair, nose, eyes, mouth, chin—but persuasive. Only a very persuasive young man could have persuaded me to ... (*Surprised by a pin-prick of memory*) Oh!

Millicent What is Alice doing?

Matilda Why doesn't she scream?

Millicent She must have been shocked as she crossed the threshold.

Matilda Was she struck dumb as she opened the door?

Millicent Coming face to face with ...

Matilda So when will she scream?

Mama (*feeling rather peculiar*) Memory seems to be returning. Like pins and needles in a foot that has been to sleep. I'm not sure that I wish to remember any more. The summer-house of all places!

Millicent So quiet.

Matilda Could he have silenced her?

Millicent Let's hope he hasn't used violence.

Matilda With more force than necessary.

Millicent Suppose ...

Matilda No, don't suppose.

Millicent What's to be done?

Matilda I can only wait.

Millicent I have been waiting.

Matilda And waiting.

Millicent And waiting.

Matilda And now

Millicent I

Matilda   can't

Millicent   wait

Matilda   any

Millicent   longer.

Millicent
Matilda } (*speaking together*) Alice!

They jump to their feet

Grandmama Was that noise necessary? Why aren't you smiling for the photographer?

Mama Why is the photographer now on his knees? In an attitude of supplication.

Millicent No reply.

Matilda Could Alice have heard?

Grandmama Could she not have heard? My ears are still ringing.

Mama (*going to the Photographer*) Is this prostration part of the photographic process, or merely an expression of desperation?

Millicent Listen?

Matilda To what?

Millicent The awful silence.

Matilda I can hear it.

Grandmama What silence?

Mama (*to the Photographer*) Could it be on account of something that was said?

Millicent Perhaps . . .

Matilda (*cutting her off*) Mere speculation.

Mama (*to the photographer*) I'm afraid I wasn't listening. At the time my thoughts were elsewhere.

Matilda She might . . .

Millicent (*cutting her off*) More speculation.

Mama (*to the Photographer*) Do stop rolling around on the grass, sir. Leave off tearing your hair and resume an upright posture.

Grandmama That girl is an unconscionable time locating my salts.

Millicent I fear . . .

Matilda The worst?

Grandmama Indeed. By the time I smell them, the need may have passed.

Mama (*to the Photographer*) You return to *your* position and we shall return to *ours*. I wish to follow my train of thought. I only hope it will not have gone without me.

As she returns to her seat the others sit. Now the twins sit together

Millicent
Matilda (*speaking together*) What is the worst you fear?

Millicent Me?

Matilda Why should I be afraid of anything?

Mama The person in the process of rearranging himself under the cover wishes us to arrange ourselves in the posture by which we would wish to be remembered by posterity. Assuming that posterity will have any interest in remembering us. Are you sitting comfortably?

Millicent } (*together to each other*) Why do you ask?
Matilda }

Mama I have no idea. It is the sort of question one asks without question. That is if your question was addressed to me—which, bearing precedent in mind, I suspect it was not.

Millicent I know what I know.

Matilda But do you know what *I* know?

Millicent What *do* you know?

Matilda Ah, wouldn't you like to know?

Millicent I might have known.

Matilda Ah. You too?

Mama I realize that what I say is counted of no importance; but judging by the way the photographer is waving his free arm, he is imploring us not to wriggle.

Grandmama Wriggle? Which of you is wriggling? Stop it at once, or we shall be stuck here all day. If *I* can control myself under difficult circumstances, so can you.

Millicent Does that include the trespasser you encountered behind the shrubbery?

Matilda I admit nothing. Though I have a clear mental picture of an interloper in the summer-house.

Millicent There has never been a gate-crasher on these premises.

Grandmama Has there not?

Millicent Certainly not in the summer-house.

Grandmama Could you swear to that?

Matilda Persons behind the shrubbery were there by invitation.

Grandmama Summer-house? Shrubbery?

Mama Mama, you appear to be making involuntary movements.

Grandmama If I did not know of all the precautions I might suspect ...

Millicent There were no assignations.

Matilda No clandestine appointments.

Grandmama The front doors are guarded, the locks on the back gates rusted fast.

Millicent Certainly no pale faced young man.

Matilda I have never set eyes on a dark moustache or side-whiskers.

Millicent Then how did you know he had a dark moustache and side-whiskers?

Matilda How did you?

Grandmama Pale face? Dark side-whiskers?

Mama Please. We are distracting the man behind the camera. (*To the Photographer*) So sorry.

Millicent Could it be ... ?

Matilda The same?

Millicent }
Matilda } (*speaking together*) It could!

Mama (*to the Photographer*) I understand. When you say, "Hold it", we do not stir.

Millicent He is there.

Matilda In the house.

Millicent }
Matilda } (*speaking together*) With her!

Mama Hold it!

Grandmama (*rising*) You ...

Millicent }
Matilda } (*speaking together*) Him

Millicent and Matilda jump up and run towards the house

Mama (*to the Photographer*) Sir! Oh, sir ...

Grandmama (*calling after the twins*) What did you see?

Mama (*watching the retreating photographer*) He is running towards the stable yard, camera held aloft and his black cloth streaming like a banner behind him.

Grandmama I do not feel well.

Mama I presume he has done what he came to do, but what a way to take his leave.

Grandmama I said I do not feel at all well. Juliet!

Mama Were you speaking to me, Mama?

Grandmama Am I looking backwards or forwards, or staring at something in front of my face?

Mama Things are happening to me, Mama. They no longer feel as though as they are happening to someone else. For the first time for so many years I am becoming involved. What can I do?

Grandmama Help me.

Mama To the house?

Grandmama Too far. Besides who knows what we might find in the house.

Mama To your chair, then.

She helps to seat Grandmama

Grandmama Do you remember a pale young man with dark side-whiskers?

Mama There must be more than one pale young man with dark side-whiskers, Mama.

Grandmama Do you remember even one?

Mama I don't want to remember ... I warned him he was trespassing; that the summer-house was out of bounds to strangers. I warned him again and again. Every time we met there. Even when he was no stranger. A most persuasive young man. Oh, how he could persuade!

Grandmama So you do ...

Mama I refuse to remember any more. Not even those sweet, stolen meetings behind the shrubbery. After thirty years how can one be expected to remember a face? Indeed, heart-to-heart, mouth-to-mouth, eyes closed by kisses, when one is ... how much does one ever *see* of a face? Oh! ... Oh, dear. How does one stop remembering?

Grandmama I only saw his face but once. Until ... Impossible! There is no way up through those petunias.

Mama If so many memories are creeping back, why is Italy not among them? Why no blue skies, romantic ruins, poetry or even spaghetti? Whatever became of the Adriatic, Mama?

Grandmama Don't press me.

Mama (*off-handedly*) Very well, Mama.

Grandmama You don't want to know.

Mama (*her tone giving the lie to her words*) If you say so, Mama.

Grandmama No good will come of it.

Mama (*unrelenting*) You know best, Mama.

Grandmama Oh, if you insist ...

Mama Yes, Mama?

Grandmama There was no villa near Venice. Only a private hotel on the outskirts of Bognor.

Mama So why distort the facts? There is no shame attached to a husband drowning off Bognor. Is there, Mama?

Grandmama Sudden twins have to be accounted for.

Mama Even to their mother?

Grandmama Especially to their mother. What a blessing you passed those nine months in a waking dream.

Mama Not only those nine months, Mama. You lied to me.

Grandmama Would you have believed me if I'd told you they'd been found under a gooseberry bush? How fortunate they do not feature their father.

Mama But they do.

Grandmama Neither Milly nor Tilly has a pale face and side-whiskers. When I look at them I am not reminded of him.

Mama I am. In duplicate. Such a ruthless, determined, utterly selfish, rather common young man. All of which, I must admit, added to his fascination. As Papa would never have agreed to a marriage, perhaps knocking the silly creature on the head was the only solution.

Grandmama I never think of him.

Mama There is no need to lie any more, Mama. I know.

Grandmama He's lost in the past. And that goes deeper than six feet of earth.

Mama The past is always with us, Mama.

Grandmama What's left of him is under the petunias.

Mama What's left of him is very much alive, Mama.

Grandmama No.

Mama What's left of him stage-managed this afternoon's comedy.

Grandmama No.

Mama What's left of him is even now in that house.

Two distant, but loud screams are heard. Grandmama half rises, then falls back, clutching her chest

I refer, of course to my bastards.

Grandmama protests inarticulately

Oh, yes, I know the word, Mama. I have never had occasion to use it, that is all. They are, though, are they not? Are they aware? Of course not. Ignorance was the guiding policy. What a pity you left me to flounder in it when a few words might have cleared that all-encompassing fog. Maybe I could have been woken only when I was ready to wake, but if only you had tried ... Then I should have less to reproach you with.

Grandmama You—me—reproach?

Mama I can understand your embarassment. Such things are not spoken of in respectable families.

Grandmama We are not speaking of them now.

Mama But if only I had been told. That missing year has hung like a shadow over all the years since. If only I had been told I might have grown into a quite different person. If only I had been told . . . But, as you say, Mama, what's past is past and now there is a future to be thought about.

Grandmama What future?

Mama The future running towards us.

The twins enter, trying to talk as they run

Millicent Agony.

Matilda Misery.

Millicent Disaster.

Matilda Calamity.

Millicent Catastrophe.

Matilda Woe.

Millicent Woe!

Mama Whoa!

The twins stand panting

Grandmama Explain yourselves.

Mama Not so much out of consideration for us, but because you will feel so much better afterwards.

Millicent They've . . .

Matilda Gone!

Millicent Along with . . .

Matilda The silver.

Millicent The jewellery.

Matilda The music boxes.

Millicent The cash boxes.

Grandmama Who?

Millicent Him.

Matilda And her.

Mama Alice?

Millicent They'll be half-way to the railway junction by now.

Matilda In the photographer's dog-cart.

Mama Is the photographer aware of that?

Millicent Who knows?

Matilda Who cares?

Millicent He should have taken ...

Millicent }
Matilda } *(speaking together)* Me!

Mama So he chose Alice. How very sensible. If only that other had been as well-advised. He and any of the other Alices would have suited each other so well—with or without the spoons.

Millicent What is to become ...

Matilda Of us?

Mama *(without looking at any of them)* That all depends upon you my dears. Personally I intend to embark, as soon as convenient, on a tour of Italy—in particular to the Adriatic shore, where I propose to seek the grave of my drowned departed and to relive the interrupted honeymoon that, until so recently, has been a blank in my life. It is now imperative that I find a husband, is it not, Mama? I shall travel alone; but what of that? As long as memory goes back—and memory now goes back further than it did—I have always been alone and talking to myself. Out there in the world who knows whom one may meet and what may be the outcome? If you really want my advice, my dears, I suggest that you adapt yourselves to circumstances, which I believe are about to improve for you. Your grandmama, to avoid the revelation of an unfortunate state of affairs which has recently come to light, has experienced a change of heart, and I predict that in future you are to be allowed access to suitable persons of the opposite gender—and Heaven have mercy on the curate! Though, while making the most of these opportunities, try to be a little less devious, especially with each other. Between yourselves deception is not only unkind but practically impossible. Adapt, my dears, is my parting advice. Accept the worst that Fate can throw at you, then turn it to your own advantage.

She turns to observe that they are staring at her, open-mouthed

Oh, my dears—have you actually been listening to me? How unusual. How gratifying. But isn't this the photographer returning? Without his dog-cart, where else was there to go? Let us dispose ourselves for him. A photograph of all four together will provide an agreeable memento. If you will sit next to me, Mama, with Millicent at one side and Matilda at the other ...

Meekly the others do as they are bid

   There. Now smile, everyone. Smile.

They smile

CURTAIN

FURNITURE AND PROPERTY LIST

On stage: Trees
               Bushes

Off stage: 2 Chairs **(Millicent)**
               2 Chairs **(Matilda)**

Personal: **Grandmama:** walking stick

LIGHTING PLOT

To open: afternoon sun in a garden

No cues

There could be a change of lighting as characters retire into their own thoughts, but this is not mandatory

EFFECTS PLOT

Cue 1   **Mama:** "What's left of him is even now in that   (Page 19)
            house."
            Two distant but loud screams

MADE AND PRINTED IN GREAT BRITAIN BY
LATIMER TREND & COMPANY LTD PLYMOUTH

MADE IN ENGLAND